MW00341158

THE BIG GOD BOOKS
The Little Church

Written by **Gabe Olson** and **Andrea Olson**
Art by **Elisa Patrissi**

For **Sophia, Adeley** and **Ayla**

We pray that these books give you
a tangible reminder that God is always working,
always for you, even if things turn out differently
than you thought they would.
May you remember there are countless miracles
happening around you every day.
And never forget to live in gratitude for them.
We love you and can't wait to continue witnessing
miracles together.
Love,
Dad and Mom

ISBN 978-1-7374374-0-6 (Hardcover Edition)
Art by Elisa Patrissi • Design by Josh Beatman/Brainchild Studios
First printing September 2021. Printed in the United States of America.
Published by Something New Publishing
somethingnewpublishing.com

Hi! I'm G!
Want to hear a little story about my **BIG** God?
Come along with me!

Welcome to my church!
My family went to this church every Sunday.
It was a little church.

It had little rooms.
And a little yard.
It had little chairs too.
But there were lots of people!

Our little church was growing.
And growing.
And growing!
I saw new people every week!

We needed more chairs for more people.
We needed bigger rooms and a bigger yard.
But building a church is a very big job.
We needed big, big,
BIG help!

So all of the people in our little church prayed.
From the biggest to the smallest.
We all prayed big prayers.

For dollars and hammers and helpers.
Because there's nothing
our **BIG** God can't do.

And guess what?
God brought the dollars and hammers and helpers!
And all the people worked together.
We built and built for many days.

I saw the helpers working hard.
I heard the hammers
pounding loud.

I saw the big cranes roll in
    to build the roof on the little church.
But then...I saw something BAD.

A big storm was coming. Oh no!
A big storm could blow the roof down!
It would ruin everything!
We had no time to get ready.
So, we prayed.
We all prayed big prayers.
Because there's nothing our **BIG** God can't do.

And guess what?
God moved the rain!
Rain fell on the left.
Rain fell on the right.
Rain fell all around.
But not a drop of rain, not a gust of wind,
not a spark of lightning hurt the little church.

It was a miracle.
Now my family goes to the new, BIG church.
And we are still growing.
But we will never forget the day God moved the rain.
Because there's nothing our **BIG** God can't do.

Start the conversation

Miracles are gifts from God. Sometimes they are the big things that we ask for. Other times, they are gifts that we didn't ask for but are exactly what we need. This story about the little church is true! We were there. We thank God every day for all the miracles we see in the world around us. The Big God Books were created to help children see the ways God works through everyday miracles.

Questions to ask

What did God do to help the people in this story? What has God done for you?

Prayer to pray

Thank you, God, for helping us in every way. I'm so grateful there's nothing my **BIG** God can't do! Amen.